After a Bath

By Aileen Fisher

Illustrated by Teresa Culkin-Lawrence

After my bath
I try, try, try,
to wipe myself
till I'm dry, dry, dry.

3

Hands to wipe

and fingers and toes

and two wet legs

and a shiny nose.

Just think how much
less time I'd take
if I were a dog
and could shake,
shake, shake.

8